Dig, Pig!

amicus
readers

Mankato, Minnesota

by Marie Powell

Ideas for Parents and Teachers

Amicus Readers let children practice reading informational texts at the earliest reading levels. Familiar words and concepts with close photo-text matches support early readers.

Before Reading
- Discuss the cover photo with the child. What does it tell him?
- Ask the child to predict what she will learn in the book.

Read the Book
- "Walk" through the book and look at the photos. Let the child ask questions.
- Read the book to the child, or have the child read independently.

After Reading
- Use the word family list at the end of the book to review the text.
- Prompt the child to make connections. Ask: *What other words end with –ig?*

Amicus Readers are published by Amicus
P.O. Box 1329, Mankato, MN 56002
www.amicuspublishing.us

Library of Congress Cataloging-in-Publication Data

Powell, Marie, 1958-
  Dig, pig! / Marie Powell.
     pages cm. -- (Word families)
  ISBN 978-1-60753-516-4 (hardcover) -- ISBN 978-1-60753-542-3 (eBook)
1. Reading--Phonetic method. 2. Readers (Primary) I. Title.
  LB1573.3.P693 2013
  372.46'5--dc23
                                2013010400

Photo Credits: Alersandr Hunta/Shutterstock Images, cover; Martine De Graaf/Dreamstime, 1; Tracey Helmboldt/Shutterstock Images, 3; Eduard Kyslynskyy/Shutterstock Images, 4, 5; Daniel Alvarez/Shutterstock Images, 6; Shutterstock Images, 9, 10, 12, 13, 15; Geoffrey Jones/Shutterstock Images, 11

Produced for Amicus by The Peterson Publishing Company and Red Line Editorial.

Editor Jenna Gleisner
Designer Marie Tupy
Printed in the United States of America
Mankato, MN
July, 2013
PA 1938
10 9 8 7 6 5 4 3 2 1

Today we are going to
the farm to get a **pig**.

We bring it home in our **rig**.

I name the **pig Zig**.

Zig loves to **dig**!

We feed **Zig** with a bottle.

He drinks a **swig** of milk.

Zig is growing **big**. We build him a pen to **dig** in.

Zig will **dig** for anything.

Even a **fig**!

We try to get **Zig** to fetch a **twig**. But he only wants to **dig**.

Zig is a fun **pig**. I wonder if we can teach him to dance a **jig**. For now I say, "**Dig, pig**!"

Word Family: -ig

Word families are groups of words that rhyme and are spelled the same.

Here are the -ig words in this book:

big
dig
fig
jig
pig
rig
swig
twig
zig

Can you spell any other words with -ig?